METALLICA

CLASSIC SONGS

OTE-FOR-NOTE TRANSCRIPTIONS WITH DVD

Transcribed by Steve Gorenberg

Cherry Lane Music Company
Director of Publications/Project Editor: Mark Phillips
Project Coordinator: Rebecca Skidmore

ISBN 978-1-60378-322-4

Visit our website at www.cherrylaneprint.com

CONTENTS

JUMP IN THE FIRE

Words and Music by
James Hetfield, Lars Ulrich
and Dave Mustaine

1st, 2nd, 3rd Verses
w/Bass Fig. 2 (3½ times)

1. Down in the depths_ of my fire - y home,_ the sum - mons bell_ will chime.___
2.3. *See additional lyrics*

Tempt - ing you and all the earth_ to

join our sin - ful kind.___ There's a job to be done_ and

I'm the one,_ you peo - ple make me do it.___ Now it's

time for your fate and I won't hes - i - tate to pull you down in - to this pit.

Chorus
w/Bass Fig. 1

So come on!___

Jump in the fire!___

So come on!_

Jump in the fire!___

3rd time to Coda

2. With

Bass Fill 1

Additional Lyrics

2. With Hell in my eyes and with death in my veins the end is closing in.
   Feeding on the minds of men and from their souls within.
   My disciples all shout to search you out and they always shall obey.
   Follow me now, my child, not the meek or the mild, but do just as I say.
   So come on! *(etc.)*

3. Jump by your will or be taken by force, I'll get you either way.
   Trying to keep the hellfire lit, I'm stalking you as prey.
   Living your life as me, I am as you see. There's part of me in everyone.
   So, reach down, grab my hand, walk with me through the land, come home where you belong.
   So come on! *(etc.)*

FOR WHOM THE BELL TOLLS

Words and Music by
James Hetfield, Lars Ulrich
and Cliff Burton

THE THING THAT SHOULD NOT BE

Words and Music by
James Hetfield, Lars Ulrich
and Kirk Hammett

9

THE SHORTEST STRAW

Words and Music by
James Hetfield and Lars Ulrich

Pulled for you.

Additional Lyrics

2. The accusations fly. Discrimination, why?
   Your inner self to die. Intruding.
   Doubt sunk itself in you. It's teeth and talons through.
   Your living catch two-two. Deluding.
   A mass hysteria. A megalomania.
   Reveal dementia. Reveal.
   Secretly. Silently.
   Certainly. In vertigo you will be. *(To Chorus)*

3. Behind you, hands are tied. Your being, ostracized.
   Your hell is multiplied. Upending.
   The fallout has begun. Oppressive damage done.
   Your many turned to none. To nothing.
   You're reaching your nadir. Your will has disappeared.
   The lie is crystal clear. Defending.
   Channels red. One word said.
   Blacklisted. With vertigo make you dead. *(To Chorus)*

WHEREVER I MAY ROAM

Words and Music by
James Hetfield and Lars Ulrich

Additional Lyrics

2. And the earth becomes my throne,
   I adapt to the unknown.
   Under wandering stars I've grown,
   By myself but not alone.
   I ask no one.
   And my ties are severed clean,
   The less I have, the more I gain.
   Off the beaten path I reign.
   Rover, wanderer, nomad, vagabond,
   Call me what you will. *(To Pre-chorus)*

HERO OF THE DAY

Words and Music by
James Hetfield, Lars Ulrich
and Kirk Hammett

Tune down 1/2 step:
④=E♭ ②=D♭
③=A♭ ①=G♭

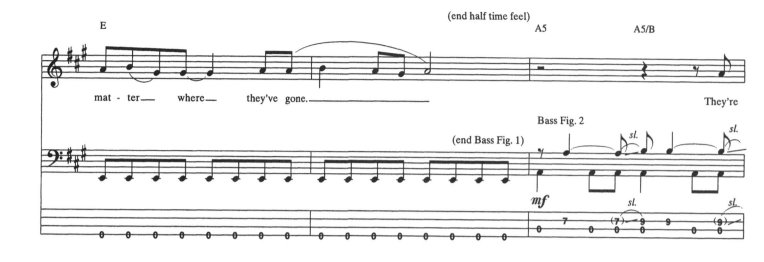

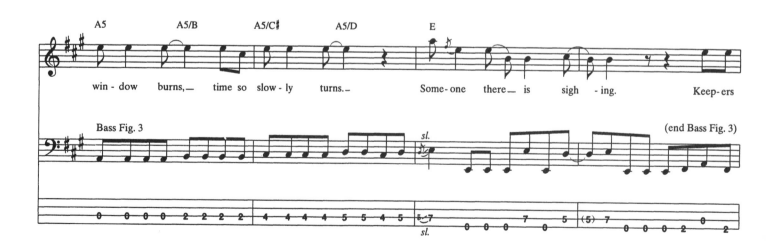

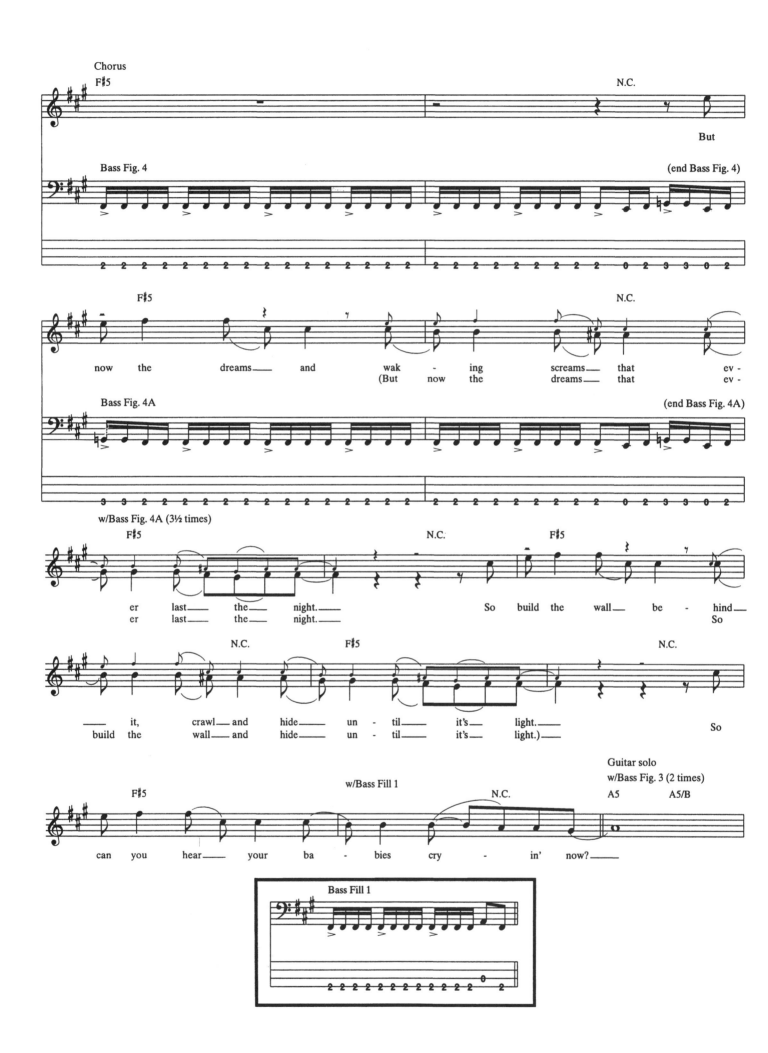

FUEL

Words and Music by
James Hetfield, Lars Ulrich
and Kirk Hammett

Tune down 1/2 step:
④=E♭ ②=D♭
③=A♭ ①=G♭

Fast Rock ♩ = 208

Intro (Band tacet)

Gim - me fuel, gim - me fire, gim - me that which I de - sire,

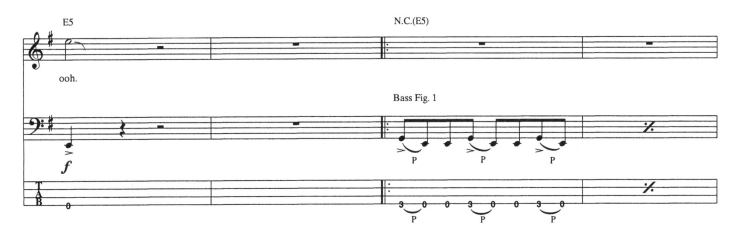

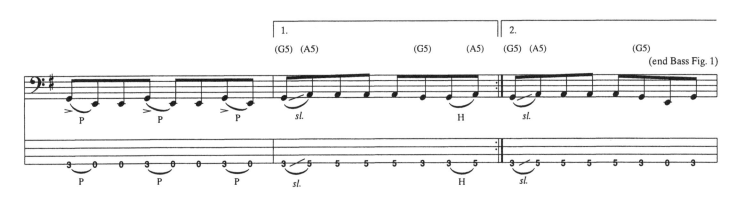

Half time feel

(A5)
Bass Fig. 2

(end half time feel)
(end Bass Fig. 2)

So gim-me fuel, gim-me fire, gim-me that which I de-sire.

Yeah.

Ooh, yeah.

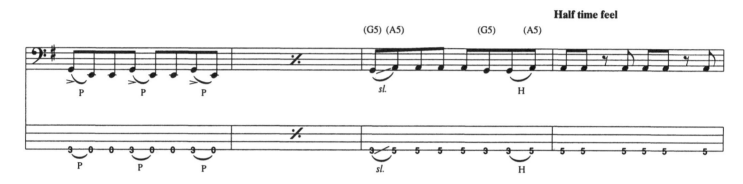

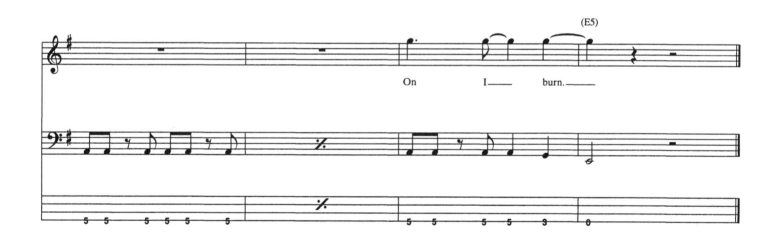

Additional Lyrics

3. Turn on beyond the bone.
   Swallow future, spit out home,
   Burn your face upon the chrome.
   Yeah, oh yeah.

4. Take the corner, join the crash.
   Headlights. (Head on.) Headlines.
   Another junkie lives too fast,
   Yeah, lives way too fast, fast, fast, woh. *(To Chorus)*

FRANTIC

Words and Music by
James Hetfield, Lars Ulrich,
Kirk Hammett and Bob Rock

5 str. drop D tuning, down 1 step:
(low to high) A-C-G-C-F

Intro

Moderately fast Rock ♩ = 168

(Guitar)

D5

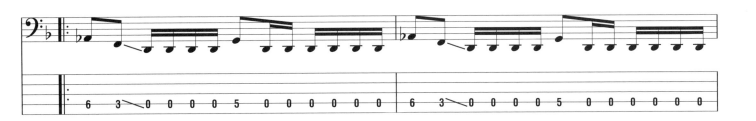

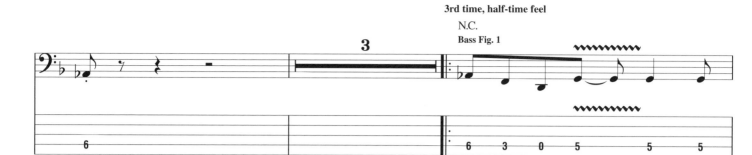

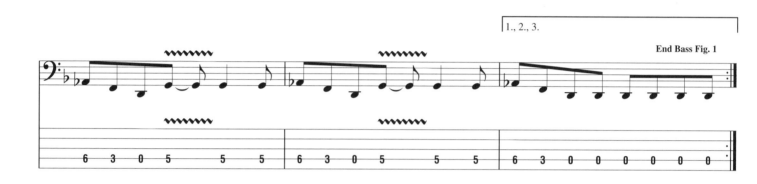

1. If I could have my wast - ed days back, would
worn out al - ways be - ing a - fraid, an

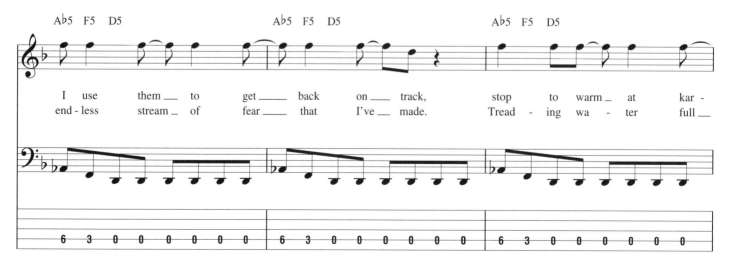

I use them to get back on track, stop to warm at kar -
end - less stream of fear that I've made. Tread - ing wa - ter full

You live it or lie ____ it! You live it or lie ____ it! (You

live it or lie ____ it! You live it or lie ____ it! My life - style de -

Bass Fig. 2

ter - mines my death - style. My life - style de -

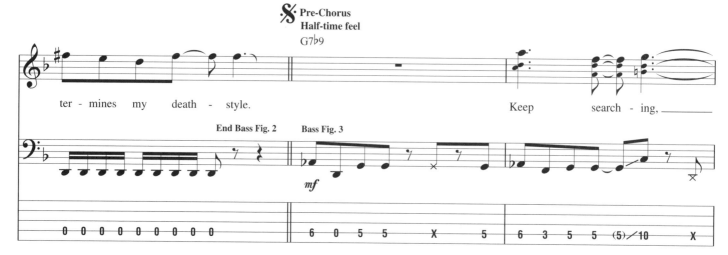

ter - mines my death - style. Keep search - ing, _____

End Bass Fig. 2   Bass Fig. 3

mf

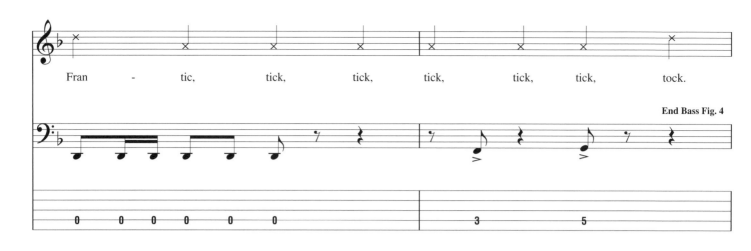

Fran - tic, tick, tick, tick, tick, tick, tock.

End Bass Fig. 4

To Coda ⊕

w/ Bass Fig. 4

Fran - tic, tick, tick, tick, tick, tick, tock. Fran - tic, tick, tick,

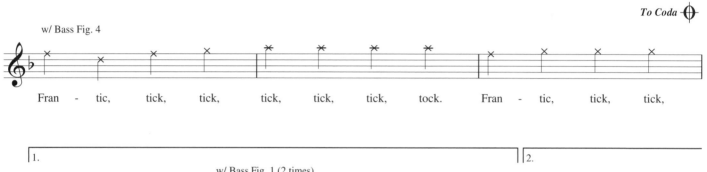

1.

w/ Bass Fig. 1 (2 times)

7

2.

tick, tick, tick, tock! 2. I've tick, tick, tick, tock!

Interlude

Half-time feel

4th time, end half-time feel

Play 4 times

N.C.

3

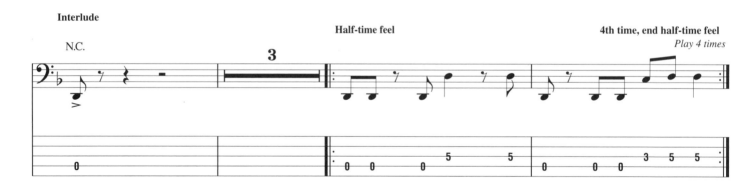

Bridge

N.C.

Do I have the strength to know how I'll go? ___

Bass Fig. 5

Can I find it in - side to deal with what I should - n't know? _____

End Bass Fig. 5

1.
w/ Bass Fig. 5

2.
w/ Bass Fig. 2 (3 times)

Oh. _____ My

D5
life - style de - ter - mines my death - style, a ris - ing tide that
(Birth is pain.

Life is pain.

F5   D5
push - es to the oth - er side. My life - style de - ter - mines my death - style, a
Death is pain.

D.S. al Coda

F5

⊕**Coda**

ris - ing tide that push - es to the oth - er side.
It's all the same.)

tick, tick, tick, tock!

Outro
Slower ♩ = 128

D5   *Play 4 times*

Play 3 times

BASS NOTATION LEGEND

Bass music can be notated two different ways: on a *musical staff*, and in *tablature*.

THE MUSICAL STAFF shows pitches and rhythms and is divided by bar lines into measures. Pitches are named after the first seven letters of the alphabet.

TABLATURE graphically represents the bass fingerboard. Each horizontal line represents a string, and each number represents a fret.

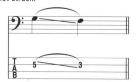

3rd string, open   2nd string, 2nd fret   1st & 2nd strings open, played together

HAMMER-ON: Strike the first (lower) note with one finger, then sound the higher note (on the same string) with another finger by fretting it without picking.

PULL-OFF: Place both fingers on the notes to be sounded. Strike the first note and without picking, pull the finger off to sound the second (lower) note.

LEGATO SLIDE: Strike the first note and then slide the same fret-hand finger up or down to the second note. The second note is not struck.

SHIFT SLIDE: Same as legato slide, except the second note is struck.

TRILL: Very rapidly alternate between the notes indicated by continuously hammering on and pulling off.

TREMOLO PICKING: The note is picked as rapidly and continuously as possible.

VIBRATO: The string is vibrated by rapidly bending and releasing the note with the fretting hand.

SHAKE: Using one finger, rapidly alternate between two notes on one string by sliding either a half-step above or below.

NATURAL HARMONIC: Strike the note while the fret hand lightly touches the string directly over the fret indicated.

MUFFLED STRINGS: A percussive sound is produced by laying the fret hand across the string(s) without depressing them and striking them with the pick hand.

BEND: Strike the note and bend up the interval shown.

BEND AND RELEASE: Strike the note and bend up as indicated, then release back to the original note. Only the first note is struck.

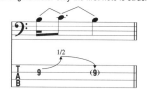

RIGHT-HAND TAP: Hammer ("tap") the fret indicated with the "pick-hand" index or middle finger and pull off to the note fretted by the fret hand.

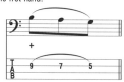

LEFT-HAND TAP: Hammer ("tap") the fret indicated with the "fret-hand" index or middle finger.

SLAP: Strike ("slap") string with right-hand thumb.

POP: Snap ("pop") string with right-hand index or middle finger.

Additional Musical Definitions

> (accent)	• Accentuate note (play it louder).
^ (accent)	• Accentuate note with great intensity.
• (staccato)	• Play the note short.
⊓	• Downstroke
V	• Upstroke

D.C. al Fine	• Go back to the beginning of the song and play until the measure marked "**Fine**" (end).
Bass Fig.	• Label used to recall a recurring pattern.
Fill	• Label used to identify a brief melodic figure which is to be inserted into the arrangement.
tacet	• Instrument is silent (drops out).

D.S. al Coda • Go back to the sign (𝄋), then play until the measure marked "**To Coda**," then skip to the section labelled "**Coda**."

 • Repeat measures between signs.

|1. |2. | • When a repeated section has different endings, play the first ending only the first time and the second ending only the second time.

NOTE: Tablature numbers in parentheses mean:
1. The note is being sustained over a system (note in standard notation is tied), or
2. The note is sustained, but a new articulation (such as a hammer-on, pull-off, slide or vibrato) begins.